Brain Games
NUMBER PUZZLES

Edward Godwin

WINDMILL BOOKS™

NEW YORK

Published in 2015 by Windmill Books, An Imprint of Rosen Publishing,
29 East 21st Street, New York, NY 10010

Text: Edward Godwin, Jane Moseley, and Jackie Strachan (JMS Books llp)
Illustrations: Memo Angeles and Others/Shutterstock
Original design concept: Notion Design
Design: cbdesign
Editors: Joe Harris with Frances Evans

Library of Congress Cataloging-in-Publication Data

Godwin, Edward.
Number puzzles / by Edward Godwin.
p. cm. — (Brain games)
Includes index.
ISBN 978-1-4777-5454-2 (library binding)
1. Mathematical recreations — Juvenile literature. 2. Puzzles — Juvenile literature. I. Godwin, Edward Xavier. II. Title.
QA95.G585 2015
513.2—d23

Printed in the United States

SL003934US

CPSIA Compliance Information: Batch #CW15WM: For further information contact Rosen Publishing, New York, New York at 1-800-237-9932

CONTENTS

PUZZLES. 4

ANSWERS. 28

GLOSSARY 32

FURTHER READING 32

WEBSITES. 32

INDEX 32

CAVEMAN CONUNDRUM

What is the missing number?

3   4   6
2   12   10
6   8   ?

RAINDROP RIDDLE

Which number completes this shower of raindrops?
(Clue: think of water spiraling around the drain!)

1   2   4
29   ?   7
22   16   11

2
6   4
20   12

3
21   6
9   15

?
45   10
20   35

IN-GENIE-OUS!

Using the first two stars as a guide, can you complete this puzzle?

ODD ONE OUT

Which number is the odd one out on the red toadstools? What about the green ones?

A 11 19 13 3 7 9 2

B 26 34 14 2 15 18 42

ALIEN ENCOUNTER

Which number is missing from the yellow segment? (Clue: look at the matching segments on each circle.)

? 3 13 4 9 6

16 1 11 2 7 4

17 2 12 3 8 5

MAKING A SPLASH

Which number doesn't go with the rest?
You can check your answer at the back.

3
9
12
6
10

4   6   2
7   17   10
3   11   ?

PIRATE PUZZLE

Can you help Cap'n Parrot work out
which number completes the scroll?

SPACE ODDITY

Look carefully at the two flying saucers and work out which number is the odd one out on each spaceship.

EGGSASPERATION!

Which of the numbers on the three eggs on the left will complete this puzzle eggsactly? (Clue: move from egg to egg in any direction.)

ANOTHER BRICK IN THE WALL

Which three-figure answer is missing from the empty brick?

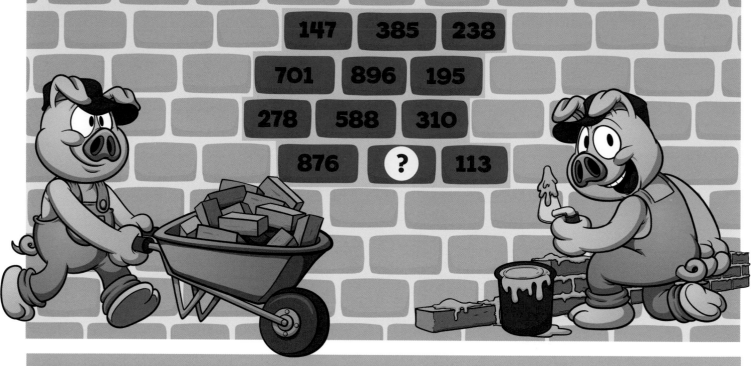

147	385	238
701	896	195
278	588	310
876	?	113

ROUGH DIAMOND

There is a rogue number in each group of gems. Can you work out which one it is? Check your answers in the back to see if you're right!

BUILDING BLOCKS

Here is a complete puzzle. Work out why the blocks contain these numbers. (Clue: the orange middle block holds the answer.)

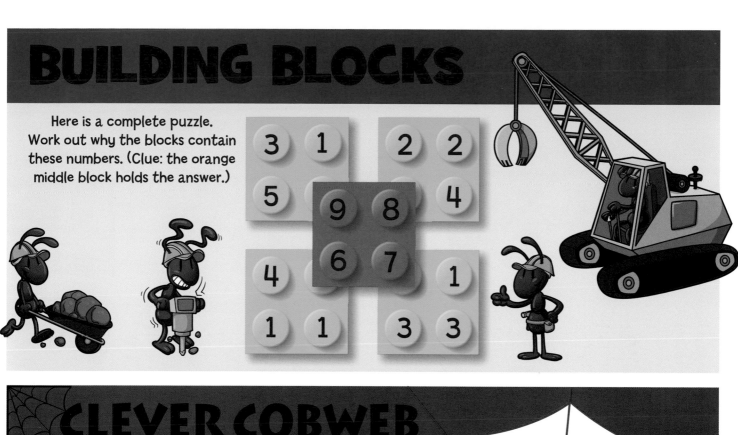

CLEVER COBWEB

Which number replaces the question mark and completes the web? (Clue: imagine rotating part of the web.)

SOCCER CRAZY

Which number completes this soccer sequence?

3 5 8 12 17 23 30 ?

PENGUIN POSER

Looking at the first two groups of penguins, can you work out which number goes on the final penguin?

RING THE CHANGES

Can you work out which number goes in the empty ring?

TRAFFIC JAM

Which number must be added to complete this sequence?

2   4   7   12   20   ?   54   88

IT'S A FRAME UP!

One number in each frame doesn't follow the same rules or requirements as all the others. Can you work out which one it is?

A
42   24   71   14   54   44

B
17   70   87   47   72   34

C
33   3   38   13   43   26

D
12   72   92   2   19   28

PICK A POSY

Which is the odd number out in each bunch of flowers?

A
12   3   9   18   15   10   6

B
7   42   28   21   35   14   25

PIECES OF EIGHT

2   5   11   23   ?

Which number should appear
on the final gold coin?

FLOWER FAIRY

Can you complete this puzzle by using
the first two flowers as a guide?

2
13   3
8   5

3
18   4
11   ?

1
8   2
5   3

5   8
?

7   4
25

6   6
33

WATCH THIS SPACE...

Using the first two planets
as an example, can you find
the missing number?

FRUITFUL FUN!

Can you complete this fruity puzzle by using the first two trees as a guide? Check your answers in the back!

MAGIC CARPET

In this puzzle we have already given you all the numbers. Can you work out why these numbers are correct? (Clue: the middle carpet is the key.)

STARFISH STRUCK

Using the first two starfish as an example, find the missing number.

BUILDING BLOCKS

Can you work out which numbers are required to complete blocks A and B?

FLOWER POWER

Can you work out the next number in this floral sequence?

WILD BILL HICCUP

Using the top two targets as an example, find the number in the empty bullet hole. You can check your answers in the back!

Target 1: 4, 3, 24

Target 2: 7, 2, 28

Target 3: 3, 8, ?

WATCH THE BIRDY!

Complete this puzzle by finding the correct number for the pink bird. (Clue: the puzzle works up and down as well as side to side!)

Row 1: 3, 4, 7

Row 2: 2, ?, 3

Row 3: 5, 5, 10

WACKY WEB

Which number do you need to add in order to complete the web? (Clue: try looking at numbers on opposite sides of the web.)

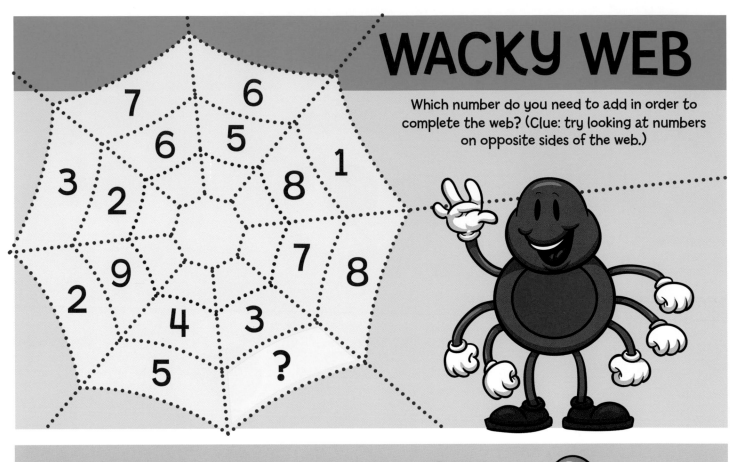

JUGGLING THE NUMBERS!

Can you explain which number on the juggler's balls is the odd one out?

NETWORK

Complete this puzzle by finishing off grids A and B, using the first grid as an example.

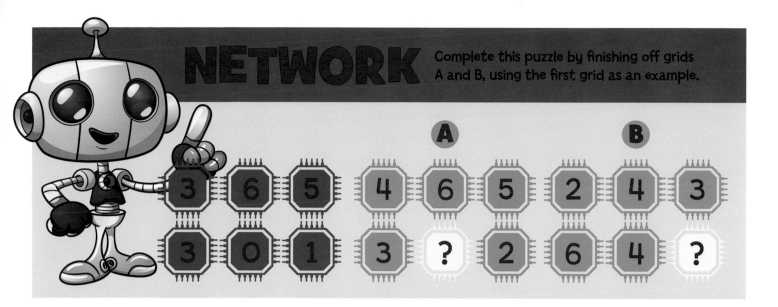

HOUSEY HOUSEY!

Using the first two houses as an example, can you work out which number is missing from the third house?

WHEEL SPIN

Which number is missing from the yellow segment in the second cog wheel? (Clue: look carefully at the matching segments in each cog.)

SOMETHING FISHY

What number goes in the middle starfish?
(Clue: it has nothing to do with adding or subtracting!)

CAKE SHOP

Can you find the correct number for the empty cupcake?
(Clue: imagine tracing a spiraling swirl in a cupcake's icing!)

JUNGLE FEVER

Which of the three numbers on the leaves on the left will complete this puzzle? (Clue: try looking up and down.)

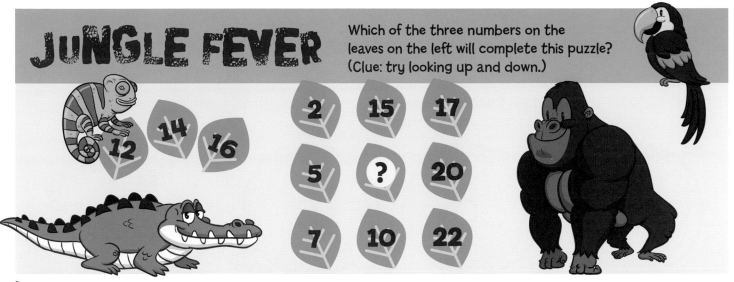

12 14 16

2	15	17
5	?	20
7	10	22

PYRAMID PUZZLER

Which number goes at the top of the third pyramid? You can check your answers in the back!

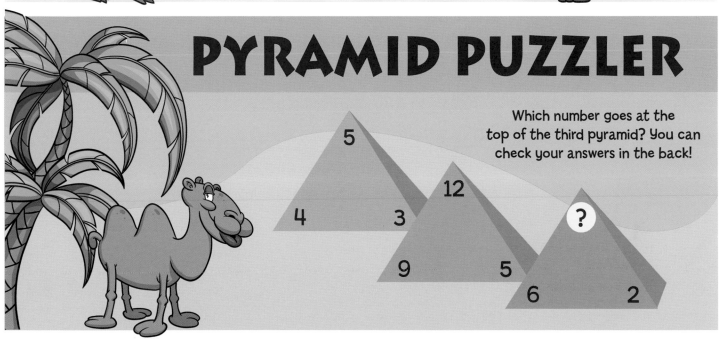

5
4   3
12
9   5
?
6   2

TAKE TIME OUT

Can you work out which number is missing from the middle clock? (Clue: look at matching segments.)

19

WHEELY TRICKY!

Using the first two wheels as an example, find the missing number.

8   3
42

9   6
45

2   7
?

CHICKEN FEED

Look carefully at the two piles of grain and work out which number is the odd one out in each pile.

A
48   64
24   55   32

B
27   41
36   63   81

2
3

5
7

?

DRAGON'S FIRE

Which number will complete this sequence?

BEE MY HONEY!

Can you work out which is the rogue number in each section of the beehive?

A — 14 9 12 18 3 6

B — 8 24 16 14 20 4

C — 12 16 24 6 36 30

D — 28 35 14 7 22 42

PARTY TIME!

Which number completes this chain of balloons? Check your answers to see if you nailed it!

3 5 9 15 23 33 45 ?

21

SHARK BAIT!

Which three-digit answer is missing from the empty fish?

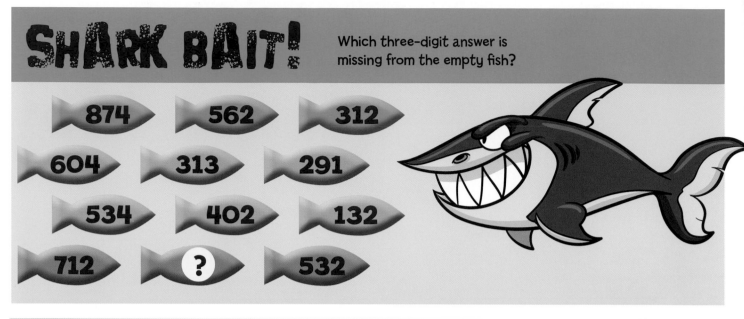

874 562 312
604 313 291
534 402 132
712 ? 532

PIZZA POSER

The first two pizzas make up the third. Can you work out what's missing? (Clue: look at the matching segments.)

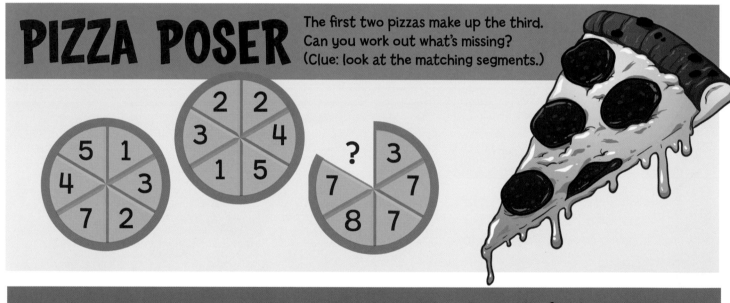

FAIRY DUST

By using the first two stars as a guide, can you complete this puzzle? (Clue: try moving clockwise.)

FRUIT SALAD

Complete this fruity puzzle by finding the missing number. (Clue: the puzzle works up and down as well as side to side!)

WITCHY WEB

Which number replaces the question mark and completes the web? (Clue: try rotating the inner section of the web...)

What number goes in the middle heart? (Clue: it has nothing to do with adding or subtracting!)

GOALS GALORE!

Using the first two soccer balls as an example, find the missing number.

CROWN JEWELS

Which number jewel doesn't go with the rest?

PEARLS OF WISDOM

Using Group A as an example, find the missing numbers.

5	7	8		B			9	8	7
3	5	6		4	9	8	5	?	3
	A			1	?	5		C	

PAPYRUS PUZZLER

Can you find the missing number on the papyrus?

2	4	5
3	2	1
6	?	5

KITTEN CAPERS

Can you work out which number goes at the top of the third pile of wool?

36
2 9

?
4 3

MONKEY BUSINESS

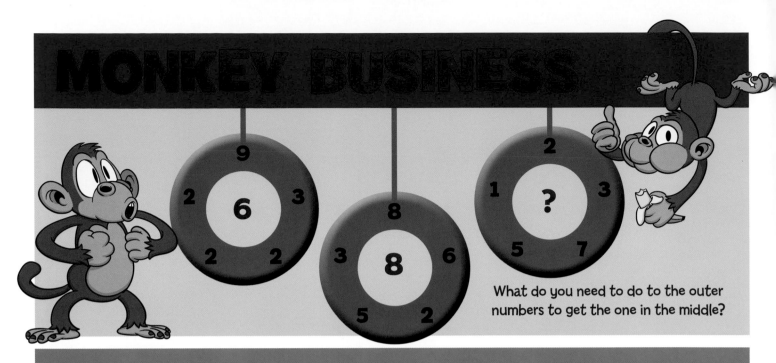

9
2 **6** 3
2 2

8
3 **8** 6
5 2

2
1 **?** 3
5 7

What do you need to do to the outer numbers to get the one in the middle?

INTERNET TROLL

Complete this puzzle by finishing off keypads A and B, using the first keypad as an example.

| 12 | 18 | 24 |
| 30 | 36 | 42 |

| 14 | 21 | 28 |
| ? | 42 | 49 |

| 16 | 24 | 32 |
| 40 | 48 | ? |

A   **B**

EASTER EGG HUNT

Which of the three eggs bottom right should replace the question mark?
(Clue: trace a pattern from egg to egg up, down, or sideways.)

2   22   29

4   16   37

7   11   ?   19   27   46

26

Complete this puzzle by adding the correct number. (Clue: try looking at the puzzle from all directions.)

WIZARD'S GOLD

8	3	4
1	5	9
6	7	?

VOLCANO MADNESS

3   12   20
   15   27

Which number is the odd one out? Don't forget to check your answers!

ANSWERS

page 4

CAVEMAN CONUNDRUM
Answer = **9**
Add the numbers on the end of each line (including diagonals) to get the middle number (12).

RAINDROP RIDDLE
Answer = **37**
Starting in the top left corner and moving around clockwise in a spiral, toward the middle, add 1, then 2, then 3, etc.

IN-GENIE-OUS!
Answer = **5**
In each star the top number will divide into the other numbers.

page 5

ODD ONE OUT
Group A = **2**
It is the only even number.
Group B = **15**
It is the only odd number.

ALIEN ENCOUNTER
Answer = **18**
Moving clockwise around each circle, starting with the lowest number, the numbers increase by 1, then 2, then 3, etc.

page 6

MAKING A SPLASH
Answer = **10**
All the other numbers are multiples of 3.

PIRATE PUZZLE
Answer = **8**
In each row and column, add the left and right hand numbers, or the top and bottom numbers, to get the result in the middle of the row or column.

page 7

SPACE ODDITY
Spaceship A = **6**
All numbers are odd.
Spaceship B = **7**
All numbers are even.

EGGSASPERATION!
Answer = **15**
Move down the first column, up the second, and down the third, adding 3 each time.

page 8

ANOTHER BRICK IN THE WALL
Answer = **989**
Add the numbers in the two outer bricks to get the number in the middle brick.

ROUGH DIAMOND
A = **11** The only odd number
B = **13** The only odd number
C = **12** The only even number
D = **16** The only even number

page 9

BUILDING BLOCKS
Add the three outer numbers in each green block to make the inner numbers in the orange block.

CLEVER COBWEB
Answer = **5**
The numbers in the inner ring have been moved on one place clockwise from the numbers in the outer ring.

SOCCER CRAZY
Answer = **38**
Moving from left to right, add 2, then 3, then 4, etc.

page 10

PENGUIN POSER
Answer = **14**
Multiply together the numbers on the two penguins on the left to get the number in the penguin on the right.
4 x 5 = 20
3 x 6 = 18
2 x 7 = **14**

RING THE CHANGES
Answer = **5**
In each row, subtract the right hand number from the left hand number to give the result in the middle ring.

page 11

TRAFFIC JAM
Answer = **33**
Start on the left and move to the right. Add the first two numbers together and add a further 1 to get the next number.

IT'S A FRAME UP!
A = **71**
All the numbers contain a 4.
B = **34**
All the numbers contain a 7.
C = **26**
All the numbers contain a 3.
D = **19**
All the numbers contain a 2.

PICK A POSY
Bunch A = **10**
It is the only number that cannot be divided by 3.
Bunch B = **25**
It is the only number that cannot be divided by 7.

page 12

PIECES OF EIGHT
Answer = **47**
Multiply each number by 2 and add 1 to get the next.

FLOWER FAIRY
Answer = **7**
In each flower, start at the top petal and move clockwise. Add the first two numbers together to give the next one along. Continue this pattern all the way around each flower.

WATCH THIS SPACE...
Answer = **37**
In each planet, multiply the two top numbers together and subtract 3 to give the bottom number.

page 13

FRUITFUL FUN!
Answer = **12**
Start with the number on the far left of each tree, and move around clockwise. The numbers increase by this far left number each time, as you go round.

MAGIC CARPET
If you add up the three numbers in each outer carpet, the total is always 10.

page 14

STARFISH STRUCK
Answer = **12**
Add up all the outer numbers in each starfish and divide the answer by 2 to get the middle number.

BUILDING BLOCKS
Answer: A = **1** and B = **8**
Taking each block individually, the top and bottom figures in each column add up to the same number.

FLOWER POWER
Answer = **128**
The numbers double at each step.

page 15

WILD BILL HICCUP
Answer = **48**
Multiply the top two numbers and double it to get the bottom number.

WATCH THE BIRDY!
Answer = **1**
Add together the first and second numbers in each row to get the third.
3 + 4 = 7
2 + **1** = 3
5 + 5 = 10

page 16

WACKY WEB
Answer = **4**
Add together pairs of numbers, one from an outer segment and one from the inner segment directly opposite. Their total should always be 10.

JUGGLING THE NUMBERS!
Answer = **23**
All the other numbers are even.

page 17

NETWORK
Answer: A = **1** and B = **5**
Add the top number to the bottom number of every column to get the same answer for each grid.

HOUSEY HOUSEY!
Answer = **16**
The number on the top window of each house equals the sum of the numbers in the other windows and doors.

WHEEL SPIN
Answer = **7**
Add together the numbers in the matching segments of the two upper wheels, putting the results in the corresponding segments of the lower wheel. So 4 + 3 = 7.

page 18

SOMETHING FISHY
Answer = **3734**
In each group of starfish, put the two figures of the number from the right hand starfish in the middle of the two figures from the left hand starfish.

CAKE SHOP
Answer = **55**
Starting in the top left corner and moving around clockwise in a spiral toward the middle, add together the previous two numbers to get the next.

page 19

JUNGLE FEVER
Answer = **12**
Moving down the first column, up the second and down the third, add 3 and then 2 alternately each step.

PYRAMID PUZZLER
Answer = **6**
In each pyramid, add together the bottom two numbers and subtract 2 to give the value at the top of the pyramid.

TAKE TIME OUT
Answer = **8**
Add together the numbers in the matching segments of the left and right hand clocks, and put the result in the corresponding segment of the middle clock (i.e. 4 + 4 = 8).

page 20

WHEELY TRICKY!
Answer = **41**
Multiply the top two numbers and reverse the figures to get the answer.

CHICKEN FEED
Pile A = **55**
All numbers are multiples of 8.
Pile B = **41**
All numbers are multiples of 9.

DRAGON'S FIRE
Answer = **11**
As you move from left to right, the numbers follow the sequence of prime numbers.

page 21

BEE MY HONEY!
A = **14**
All the rest are multiples of 3.
B = **14**
All the rest are multiples of 4.
C = **16**
All the rest are multiples of 6.
D = **22**
All the rest are multiples of 7.

PARTY TIME!
Answer = **59**
Moving from left to right, add 2 to the number in the first balloon to get 5, then add 4 to this to get 9, then 6 to get 15, adding an extra 2 at each step.

page 22

SHARK BAIT!
Answer = **180**
In each set of three fish, subtract the number in the fish on the right from the number in the fish on the left, to get the number in the middle.

PIZZA POSER
Answer = **7**
Add together the numbers in the matching segments of the first two pizzas on the left, and put the answer in the corresponding segment of the third pizza (i.e. 5 + 2 = 7).

FAIRY DUST
Answer = **12**
Starting with the top number and moving around clockwise, add 1 to get the next number, then 2, then 3, etc.

page 23

FRUIT SALAD
Answer = **6**
Multiply together the first and second numbers in each horizontal line to get the third.
2 x 3 = 6
3 x 1 = 3
6 x 3 = 18

WITCHY WEB
Answer = **3**
The numbers in the inner ring have been moved on one place clockwise, from the numbers in the outer ring, with 1 subtracted.

page 24

LOVE BUGS...
Answer = **2678**
Taking all four figures in the first and last hearts, put them in numerical order in the middle hearts.

GOALS GALORE!
Answer = **15**
On each ball, multiply together the numbers on the left and the right, and divide the result by 2 to get the middle number.

CROWN JEWELS
Answer = **44**
All the other numbers in the row are square numbers.

page 25

PEARLS OF WISDOM
Answer: B = **6** and C = **4**
In group B, the bottom number is 3 less than the top number; in Group C it is 4 less.

PAPYRUS PUZZLER
Answer = **8**
Work down through the papyrus in columns. Multiply the top number by the middle number to get the bottom number.

KITTEN CAPERS
Answer = **24**
In each group of three balls of wool, multiply the bottom two numbers and double the result to get the top number.

page 26

MONKEY BUSINESS
Answer = **6**
Add up the outer numbers and divide by 3 to get the middle numbers.

INTERNET TROLL
Answer: A = **35** and B = **56**
In the first keypad, starting with the first number on the left in the top row, moving across to the right, 6 is added to each previous number. Using the same pattern, 7 is added to each previous number in keypad A, and 8 in keypad B.

EASTER EGG HUNT
Answer = **46**
Move down the left hand column, then up the middle, and down the right hand column. Start by adding 2 to the first number, then add 3 to the next number, then 4, 5, etc., all the way around.

page 27

WIZARD'S GOLD
Answer = **2**
The numbers create a magic square, in which the numbers along any vertical, horizontal, or diagonal line add up to 15.

VOLCANO MADNESS
Answer = **20**
All the other numbers are multiples of 3.

GLOSSARY

conundrum (koh-NUN-drum) A riddle or puzzle.

encounter (en-KOWN-tuhr) A meeting you did not expect to have.

ingenious (in-JEE-nee-us) Very clever or cunning.

keypad (KEE-pad) An arrangement of keys for typing.

papyrus (pah-PY-ruhs) Paper made from the papyrus plant, used by Ancient Egyptians.

pyramid (PIH-rah-mid) A royal tomb built by Ancient Egyptians, with a square base and four triangular sides.

requirements (ree-KWYR-muhnts) Things that are wanted or needed.

sequence (SEE-kwuhns) An arrangement of things in a particular order.

volcano (vol-KAY-noh) An opening in the Earth's crust that allows hot rock, ash, and gas to escape.

FURTHER READING

Connolly, Sean. *The Book of Perfectly Perilous Math*. New York: Workman, 2012.

Harbin-Miles, Ruth, Don Balka, and Ted Hull. *Math Games*. Huntington Beach, CA: Shell Education, 2013.

Pearson, Kelli. *Miss Brain's Cool Math Games, Level 2*. New York: BrainSpark, 2013.

WEBSITES

For web resources related to the subject of this book, go to:

www. windmillbooks.com/weblinks and select this book's title.

INDEX

aliens 5
animals 8, 9, 10, 19, 24, 25, 26
balloons 21
bees 21
birds 7, 10, 15, 20
cakes 18
cars 11
cavemen 4, 20, 27
clocks 19
dragon 20
fish 14, 18, 22
flowers 11, 12, 23
houses 17
magic carpet 13
pirates 6, 12
soccer 9, 24
space 7, 12
spiderweb 9, 16, 23
trees 13